We introduce you to Patricia (Trish) Frech, who has published a collection of poetry that transforms moments of nature or events into philosophic or iconic scenes taking the reader on musical or natural journeys. Patricia recently retired from teaching to complete this work; her role as a teacher, professor and lover of nature is the backdrop of her prosaic, musical, and philosophic eye as seen through various genres such as odes, riddles, songs, sonnets and iconic lyrical poetry. Trish transforms silence into revelations of human nature. Her backdrop is one of literary and personal journeys: a teacher in secondary and college classrooms; a traveler from her home town in Virginia, to a cultural education in Hawaii; teaching in private and public schools in Maine, Hawaii, and Virginia, and an immersion of British schools on a sabbatical in England. You will want to travel with her as her book covers three arenas and ends with an appendix that is both instructional and personal as she lays out some protocols for students or teachers to use in the classroom. *Writers, Like Hats* opens with an ode and ends with students' profound view for the future.

I dedicate this book to my parents, Clarence and Julia Jane Vellines and also to my husband , Lloyd (Pete) Frech. Without their support for my continuing education, and personal support, this book would not have been possible.

Professors who encouraged my pursuit of composition and poetry:

Robert Pack: Bread Loaf School of English, poetry professor, Middlebury College.

Martin Price: Bread Loaf School of English, Middlebury: professor at Yale University.

Gordon Donaldson: Advisor, educational leadership, University of Maine.

Students who inspired me by their enthusiasm.

Colleagues who encouraged my interest and love of poetry:
Their names are too numerous to list,
Their infinite willingness *to write on, write on, write on…*

Patricia Frech

WRITERS, LIKE HATS

AUSTIN MACAULEY PUBLISHERS™

LONDON • CAMBRIDGE • NEW YORK • SHARJAH

Ordering Information
Quantity sales: Special discounts are available on quantity purchases by corporations, associations, and others. For details, contact the publisher at the address below.

Publisher's Cataloging-in-Publication data
Frech, Patricia
Writers, Like Hats

ISBN 9798889100386 (Paperback)
ISBN 9798891551251 (Hardback)
ISBN 9798889100393 (ePub e-book)

Library of Congress Control Number: 2023917333

www.austinmacauley.com/us

First Published 2023
Austin Macauley Publishers LLC
40 Wall Street, 33rd Floor, Suite 3302
New York, NY 10005
USA

mail-usa@austinmacauley.com
+1 (646) 5125767

My thanks to the following for their technical assistance:

Lloyd R. (Pete) Frech – photography

Daniel Gover – computer adviser

Kate Gover – editing, proofreading, photo sizing

Table of Contents

Writers, Like Hats

Soft, conforming to era and form
Wrapping wisdom in the comfort of age
Wide-brimmed and stiff confronting the norm

Bright, bold, and unique, dispelling gloom
Sassy, surreal, sensuous, swimming against the tide
Hiding frailty of youth or age,
Framing an ageless rhyme

Underneath, caged, yet born to unwind
A mystery of magic: driven by imagery and sound,
A stroke of a pen or touch of a key
Unleashes the script of humanity

A treasure, held hostage to pattern
A weaver of words enfolded and smothered
In rain pouring down, a new voice is born

Ode to the Inkpen

O little pen, thou willow reed,
What wisdom dost thou say?
You glide along a strong coarse grain
Yielding and bending my way.
Your mold is oh so narrow and thin!
Your grasp is oh so chill!
Your path finds constancy in my mind
You pause, and I refill.
On me, your guide, you must depend
And I on thee must wait,
For who but thee, oh willow reed,
Can clarify my fate?
The porous ore that gives you life
Was fashioned from the earth,
As thoughts that spill into that shaft
Are funneled from my soul

Section-I
The World of Nature

THE WORLD

OF

NATURE

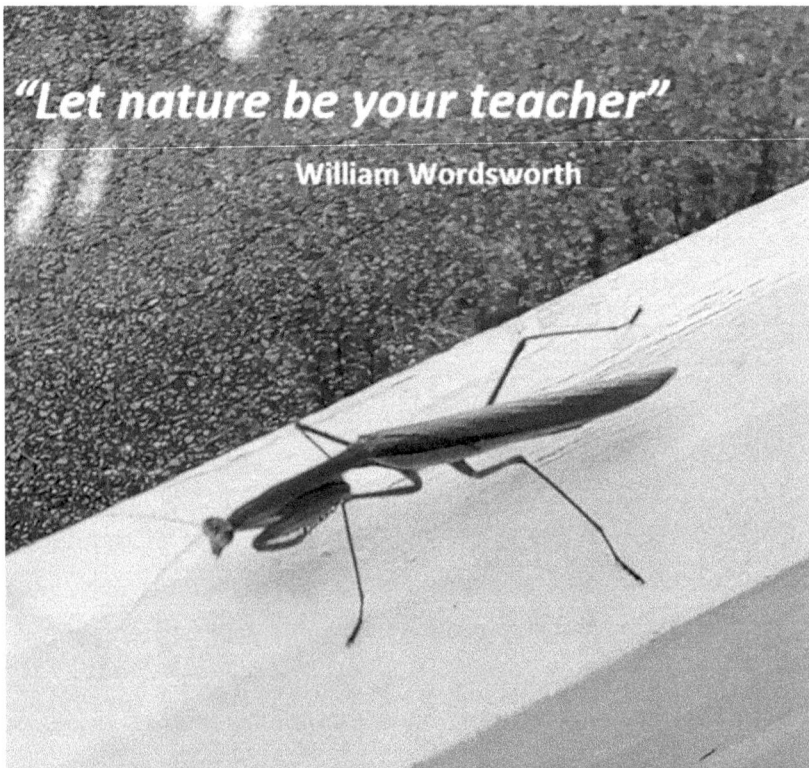

"Let nature be your teacher"

William Wordsworth

Rhythm of Nature

From shadows of night to checkerboard light
Sights, sounds awaken the day
A carpet of darkness opens its green:
A screen of tiny flickers
Engaging leaves to open their space.
    Insects, animals and birds in flights.
    A kitty curled up begins its yawn
    Cleaning and bathing in nature's soft earth.
    A tiny ant hops to pick up a crumb
    While the hawk overhead circles its prey.
        A pattern of white stretches its cape
        Opening and closing an ocean of blue.
        A soft yellow light spreads its rays from the East
        While life on the earth awakens to day.
A bike whizzes by with a whiff of air
The roar of an engine grinding its path.
The rhythm is faster; the voice calls deeply
The bodies crochet in a garment of clay
Molding and moving along their way.
    A screech or a yell pulls the garment apart
    Creating a vacuum of discord: an engine of fear
    Whistles and bells sound an alarm
    While animals and birds flee to their nests.
        All nature reacts in a web of distrust
        Expanding and closing and tightening the cord
        That binds and protects the cycle of life.

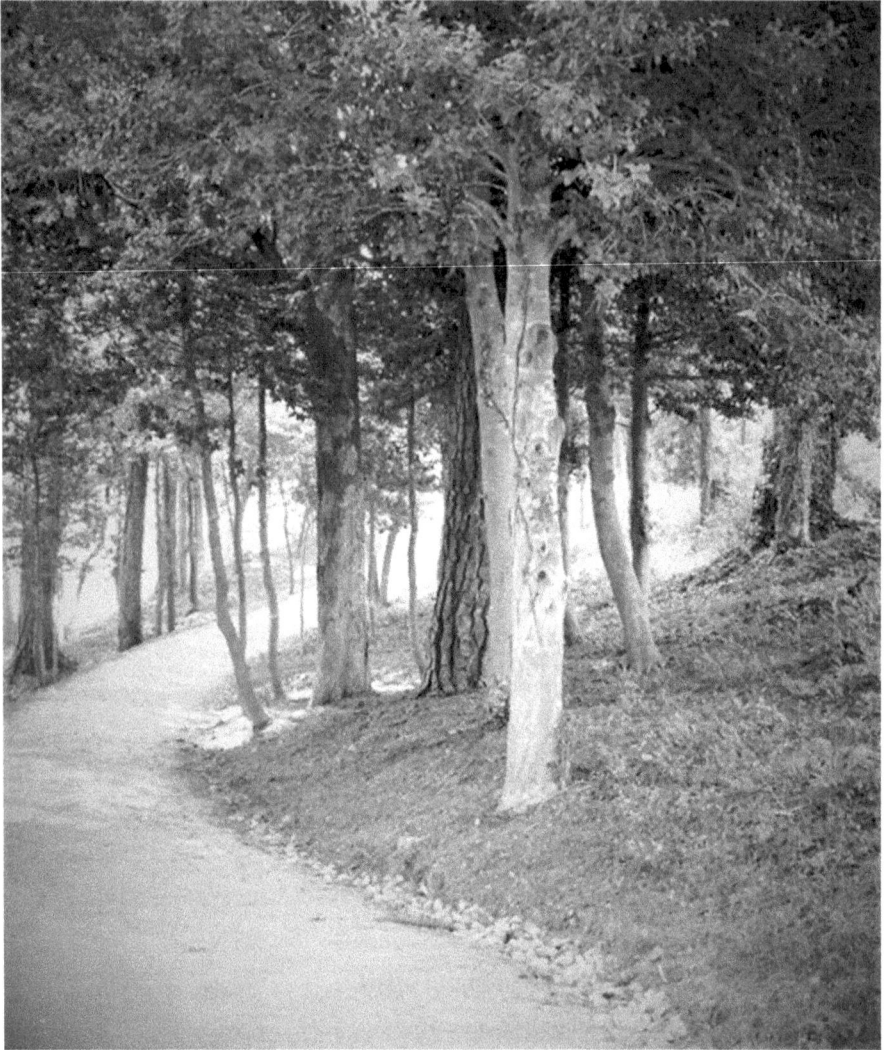

A MOUNTAIN PATH
ON MY MORNING STROLL……

In the Silence of the Morn

Filters surreal with jagged snips of yesterday
Fade into papier-mache images
Rough with edges of color and tints fading
Eyelids snapping the daylight lens

Toes pushing aside the blanket of night
Tingling nerves held hostage in the sheets so tight
Soft breaths signal a rebirth of muscle and might
While the body unwinds like a hinge upright

Stretching and reaching, impulses ignite
Gathering motion into movement and sound
A sigh, a valve seeps into a motionless silhouette
Pale with the sketch of day.

Amidst the dew and soft earth
The grass shakes its arms
The bee lifts its wings
As the movie begins…
A new day is born
Out of the silence of morn.

The Dawn

The dawn approaches with her rusty hue
    Announcing birth of day with harps of sound
    That play upon the misty ears of sleep
    To stretch and bend the muscle of the night
    Binding fears and tangling daytime scenes.
        Unevenly, her cords unwind the morn
        And sew the strands of light around the clouds.
        Her breath plays hide-and-seek amongst the hills
        Then muffles doves that come to rest;
        They warble softly, perched upon a roof.
            Her breezy notes float upward from the lake
            To tantalize the leaves and lift the buds
            Who open up their throats to catch the hum
            Of crickets folding up the shades of night.
                The swelling tenor voices of the birds
                Fan upward from the bass of ponds and heath
                To prick the dreams of spiders on the green
                Whose folded moths lie trapped in nighttime's tomb.
The chorus of the night—a patterned clue
To petals brushed with morning's crimson dew.

A Stroll with Wordsworth

This poem began six decades ago, then remerged when I spent several weeks in the Lake District in England, visiting Wordworth's home, school, and Dove Cottage. Then the memory returned as I recently began my morning walks in my birthplace.

A woody knoll breaks through the brush
Of a mountain path on my morning stroll.
The August air breathes heavy
As leaves and branches keep me company
In this sacred place where I worship
Wordworth's voice.
Below, a herd of sheep graze within the stone wall
On either side of the path.
This is munching time.
There are no travelers, save me.
My silent song, a careful note
In my symphony of memories
Jotted down at end of day
To capture images to share in years ahead.
The wonder and power of this giant of verse
The stillness of this view, forever
Carved in my tiny soul.
How great thou art; beside the hue of morn
And the span of this walking trail.
You take me back to another trail
In the mountains of Virginia
On an Eastern morn long ago:
I walked alone that summer up a narrow trail,
Carefully pacing the narrow path

To a seat on a stone overlooking
A peak of Masanutten mountain range.
The midst of clouds opened slowly
Like a camera with a panorama view.
I could not speak; I could not sing;
I quietly absorbed a moment of joy.
With my amateur brush and pencil
In hand, one-dimensional in size
Was all I could retain of heaven's view.
Years rolled by; these two moments merge
Now in the voice of my soul,
Folding together to recapture the bliss,
And power of poetry.

Where Is the Shepherd?

In the early morn, a soft mist rises
Leaving its coat underneath the towering trees
Sheep nestled in the warmth of autumn's breath
New shorn coats open to the eastern breeze
Where is the Shepherd?
Gathering a pail of mulch to mix the morning meal
So deftly did he move with buckets in each hand
Whistling to his canine following closely at his heel.
Each measured step timed to reach the herd upon the hill.
Then a shadow in the ashen sky betrayed the peaceful scene
Diving straight into a wandering ewe
A falcon's dive, swift and sharp, split the heavy air
Breaking the silence of nature's ear.
Where is the shepherd when danger is near?
Outside the warmth and comfort of the herd.
Alone and forlorn, grieving a wooly victim's fate.
At break of day, sheep are huddled close
Blinded by sunlight, looking straight ahead,
And following closely, a lamb without its ewe.

A Seed Bursts into Flower

A seed bursts into flower—
    Filling the air,
    Bending to touch
    A honeybee,
    Yielding to the sting
    Of nature's hour.
I envy the power
    Of that tiny bee,
    Flitting carefree,
    Storing up the gift
    Of pleasure
    Succulently.
A sweetness stored
    By community work,
    None shirking
    Social degree.
    Each building
    A pattern
    Delicately.
Each hive alive
    With energy,
    Following a queen,
    Carefully
    Watching her
    Majesty.
A simple task,
    A light command.

A taste of honey
  In my hand.
I cower and flee,
    Avoiding the sting
    Naturally.

Flowers

I

Seed, bud, and you
    Blossomed into air;
A burst of yellow and brown,
    Tearing away a frown
Opening up a slender smile
Daring the sun to pluck a hair.

II

One day I picked a perfect rose
    Took it for my own,
Regarding not the hand from which
    The seeds were sown.

III

Tossed it in my strands of hair
    About my face, into my skin.
It shed a rainbow glow,
    A lacquer smooth and thin.

IV

The perfumed air surrounded me
    Took away my breath
Then velvet curls split and burned,
    Consuming me with death.

V

Touch not the thing you love too well;
　　Control the passion, a deadly shell.

When the Lilacs' Bloom

When the lilacs' bloom,
The breath of summer
Hugs the Earth.
The sun spreads out its arms
Sprinkling bumble bees
Upon vines, spilling nectar.
Nature's wine fills the air:
The pace moves slowly
From dawn till dusk
Lifting a morning sigh
To a silhouette of night
Billowing clouds chasing the West Wind
In a fiery blaze at end of day.

Leaves

Unfolding, open to warm air
Inviting nature's songbirds to nest.
Time of rebirth
Open to the wind, coats of green
Wrapping slender arms, reaching for the sky
Framing meadows, alive with bees, butterflies and insects.
Glorious chorus from the throat of earth
Rumbles in the air, rolls across fields
Lifting the breath of spring.

LISTEN............
Whistling birds; hoot of the owl,
Buzzing of wings; dust dripping its yellow grain
Feeding the fields.
Night drops its honey dew,
Pumps its sacred water through thirsty soil.
Nothing can stop the cycle;
No one can steal its gold.
It rolls a mighty band from east to west:
Never missing a day of work;
Never failing to follow the rules;
Never snapping the chain of life.
Follow the leaves
Release the voice
Lift up and SING!

Defiant Rose

In the midst of winter
Leaves of my trailing body
Freeze my blood, halting my strength
Leaving me crippled and drab.

Air stifled with winter's breath
Tiny Tits and hungry cardinals
Ravage seeds from icy limbs.
Hugging my body, pushing from inside
I seek entry into a frozen world.

Facing the wind,
I peer into a hollow haven
Patches of nature's rain
Cracking my vein

A face behind the windowpane
Taps lightly through the glass
Searches for signs of life.

A pink bud pierces my skin,
Unfolding a dusty hue
Proud, bold, and firm
I defy the gray of winter's face.

The Gate

The leaves of fall: frail, fighting winter's grasp
Holly huddled in the warmth of soil
Alone they guard the skeleton forest
Inviting Nature's frosty breath.

Today, they welcome an iron gate
Whose arms closed to invaders
Stands braced to hold the gentle doe
Nibbling the sweet, deep green of moss and fern.

The nod of motion signals an unwelcome guest
Intruder from the other side...
A turn, a leap – a slight brush of air
"No Entry", whispers the Gate.

When the Wind Is Blowing

When the wind is blowing
Limbs reach out their arms
Bending and waving
Rustling a tune

Listen quietly to Nature's song
A message of darkness or light
A whirl dancing
Between joy and pain.

A cloud unfolds its heavy load
Descending drips of gold
Flooding the earth
Restoring the green.

With patience and calm
A cycle of life
Restores its own
On a windy morn.

The Ballet Dancer

Soft, quiet dusk
Beckons the wardens
Along the marsh
    In the mezzanine
    I gaze into the stillness
    At end of day.
        In the corner of my window
        A glimpse, a shadow
        Taps lightly over the pink pavement
        Nose poised; dark eyes fixed
        Still…A tan body turning, reaching
            One elegant leap
            The ballet dancer glides
            Forward, small antlers sculpted beside each ear
            A young buck, alert, curious, pirouetting
            Ears parallel, tight body, spiraling
            Nano-seconds, tiny leaps. Head swirling
            Landing five paces from the magnolia
            His head darts around, up, down
            Smelling gardenia, surveying his stage
                Like a swan on a lake
                    Across the lawn's edge
                    Lapping dark green leaves
                    As the curtain falls
                    Frozen in eventide: his audience spellbound.

Cycle of Life

Spiders
Build webs
Design, extend, capture, feed
Birds build a safe place, procreate
Teach young to fly and search for food
Animal kingdom – find safety, search for food
Search for mate, feed, train young for life, survival.
Humans search for mate, unite for birth, nourish young.
Build protection, trust, follow rules, educate, move from family.
Step beyond and build community, expand outside, create unique body
Develop mindset, plan, organize goals, experience independence, foster inner circle
Learn to be independent, look ahead, reach out, change, face obstacles and accept failures
Journey through valleys, climb hills, reach apex, survey plateau, expand and select perimeters
Build on lessons from the past, strive for renaissance, reflect needs, reshape, establish peace.
Step off ledge with comfort and knowledge, descend and accept greener pastures for future
Recognition and responsibility for decision-making, select values from the past.
Ascending to glory of life or descending to abyss: FREEDOM IS CHOICE
No middle ground

Section-II
The World Outside

VIOLENCE ERUPTS

NATURE'S FIRE

TURMOIL OF
JUSTICE AND FEAR

VOICES OF
IRE RISE
AGAIN AND AGAIN

The World Outside

Hovering over my world
Violence erupts in cities
Nature's fire rises in mountains, quakes, and rain.
Protestors making their voices heard
Midst the turmoil of justice and fear
No voice can calm the ire that rises again and again
In a land where peace and prosperity were sacred

Where is the calm rhetoric of reason?
Where are the makers of governance and common sense?
Every word, every image filled with the poison of hate.
In the midst of nature's wrath, pandemic splits us apart.
The ease of social consciousness slips beyond our reach.
Fear of friends and family – the masque of plague
Mirrors faces broken by deadly air.

Drive beyond the city's bleak shadow
Out to the vales of Nature's forests and fells…
There with the cattle, sheep, roosters and hens
The little lamb stands alongside the cow
Unaware of feature or gene,
He munches beneath the horns of the bull.
Lies down beside chicks and their clan.
Then snuggles beneath a pig and its trough.
There in the midst of oats and straw,
Is the warmth of nature's smiling voice
"Come unto me my child, awaken to the peaceful
Arms that stretch beyond the walls of hate;
Forget and forgive wars of yesteryear

Meet me in the pasture, green with the coming of spring.
There you may jump with joy and delight
In the midst of creatures standing with strangers
Embracing and enhancing life without strife
Let go of the past, play host to all breeds
Mingle and munch among strangers and friends
The shadows of shame and remorse lie buried
In clogs of mud and marrow of dirt
Buried..."

The World Outside

Ode to the Midnight Prowler

I

Pepper roams at night
Wild and free, her territory framed
Within a tiny lane.
Her black coat and golden eyes
Lure neighbors…purring softly
As she weaves in and out of reach.

II

As day breaks, beneath the portico
She arrives, climbing atop the granite steps
Patient, attentive, a perfect picture of a gentle child.
Her adopted parents read her every move
Bowls of treats, ice cubes gently moving in humid air
She waits for a soft palm to rub her neck.
At daybreak, the innocent face awaits.

III

In between dawn and dusk
Pepper roams: chasing victims large and small
Jumping, running, hiding underneath the ivy ropes
Waiting for her prey.

IV

The afternoon glow brings her back
Heavy breathing and glossy eyes
Define her, guide her once more

To await parental hug and smooth rub
Of caretakers, blessed with the gentle
Touch of her fur and warmth of her body.

V

Moving in and out, the silent language of
The prodigal returning home
Closes the day
Welcoming the wandering child with no remorse.

Pepper Is My Name

Pepper is my name
I roam the neighborhood
Visiting houses on my lane.
For the moment, I am sitting
On the porch, in her rocking chair.
The two who live here give me food
Every day and I want to go inside.
I tried the back door last week
I scampered in to pass through
And she opened the front door for my exit.
I like being here but I also like to roam
I'm just a young kitty, playing and hiding
Are my pastimes every day.
But today, I slipped in the front door
He picked me up and set me outside.
I want to stay, and I know they
Care about me. They talk to me;
They give me special attention
Only they are not my owner;
Being a community kitty is confusing.
I want to belong, but my owners
Are not there when I need them.
My neighbors fill the time with
Food and lots of love.
What to do?

Caretakers of the World

Unseen, they welcome a giant task
In floods, tornadoes, fire, disasters of the weak and homeless
They climb the peaks, drive into hostile environments
Render services for impossible remnants of cities, towns,
Holes in the earth.
They appear without a call, give comfort amid a raging nation.
They give to helpless, forgotten souls who walk the earth.
A shadow of humanity – voices soft but tone is clear
Invisible to the crowd, powerful to a weeping heart.
They walk away without a trumpet,
Their voices are eternal.

Alone

Waiting for the morning sun
Creeping through the curtains – pushing back the dawn
Hoping to hear silence from the knell of death
Leaning into the latest forecast
Watching the red lines rise or drop
Listening to cackle of birds, sending a signal to the nest.

A New Day

Bringing the scent of daffodils
Lifting up their arms for air, waving their golden hair
To a puff of wind and a shift of earth
Untouched in the face of morn. Untarnished in the birth of day
Caressing the grassy slope.

The Curtain Lifts

Dripping with morning dew
Color dazzles the weary traveler
Plodding over the hill Into the Valley below
Shoes shifting the dirt beneath the trodden sole
Scratching the heel that bends to the sand and dust
Of Yesterday's Plow.

Silence in between each step...Bent forward...

*Poised to whisper...*To the open Air: **HOPE**

Legacy Of Shakespeare, April 23rd

I

That time of year when rain is soft and warm
And windy breezes blow the budding trees
My mind becomes a buzzing, hazy swarm,
Alert, yet inattentive: nature's freeze.
The sounds of spring surround me with their glee
The birds returning to their empty nests.
The squirrels romp and play beneath the tree,
Delighted with the crumbs of winter's fest.
The cracks and holes from nature's tiny beasts
Are dotted over lawns and fields now bare.
Still underneath they gather round a feast
Preparing for their move through springtime's tear.
Not one complains that food is sparse and stale,
They humbly come together, strong, yet frail.

II

That time of year when showers come and go
And springtime flowers show their budding face
Our thoughts return to someone long ago
Whose heritage is something we embrace.
His name is linked to tragedy and tears
To lovers' joys and frolics in the night
To triumph, failure, suffering and fears
His world became a stage of human light.
And every year he speaks through youth and age

To join our common hearts in drama's art
That breathes a language spoken on a stage
Where we together mend our broken hearts.
The gift of William Shakespeare joins our hands
Across the oceans, continents and lands.

III

Today we celebrate a great man's birth.
His heritage of verse endures through time,
Reminding us that life upon this earth
Is beautiful expressed in flowing rhyme.
We learn from Hamlet what we each must face –
Our common grief, our fate, our endless fear,
And centuries of time cannot erase
"To be or not to be" from mankind's ear.
When poets speak, their wisdom is the seed
To help us love or smile or quell our hate.
They fall into our hearts in times of need
Enabling us to seek our natural fate.
This language that we use is just a tool
To help us to be kind when life is cruel.

WAR – A Hole in the World

– A Tribute to President Zelensky

War, a hole in the world
Shredding apart stich by stich,
With every move, connections
Tearing one body from another.
A nation crumbling from a meteor
Forcing its threads to scatter, split
Energy, power, darkness
Pulling seams of family, friends
A needle of strength, a voice from within
Bold, compassionate, strong
Weaves among the weeping dead
In and out of fallen buildings
Mending minds, resonating
Far and Wide
The garment of freedom.
Tattered, fragile, wavering
Images pull at borders
A string of hope to bandage the world
"Freedom is but choosing" – War or Peace?

March 16, 2022

Ode to the Queen – A Piper's Final Note

A single tear from a son's heart
A great-granddaughter shedding tears at day's end
A loyal family walking steady behind a coffin
Miles of mourners lining the royal cavalcade
Silent nation: millions frozen motionless in honor
A Cinderella marriage blessed with joyful legacy
<u>Memoir of images</u> – A young woman called to serve amidst an angry world
A family monarch guiding a nation and family
A wise listener holding the reign of country, family, staff, horse and puppies
A model for us all: leaving behind a smile, a message of peace and good will,
Sense of humor, patience and gentle voice
At end of day…a legacy that resounds beyond the grave
Her audience: the meek and great
A piper sounding chords through the doorway to eternity
That all of us will face.
May her walk stir our world to climb together to the Apex of worldwide peace.
September 19, 2022

Section-III
The World Inside

Memories

Dreams

Growing Up

The Classroom

Songs of Youth

Graduation

The Web

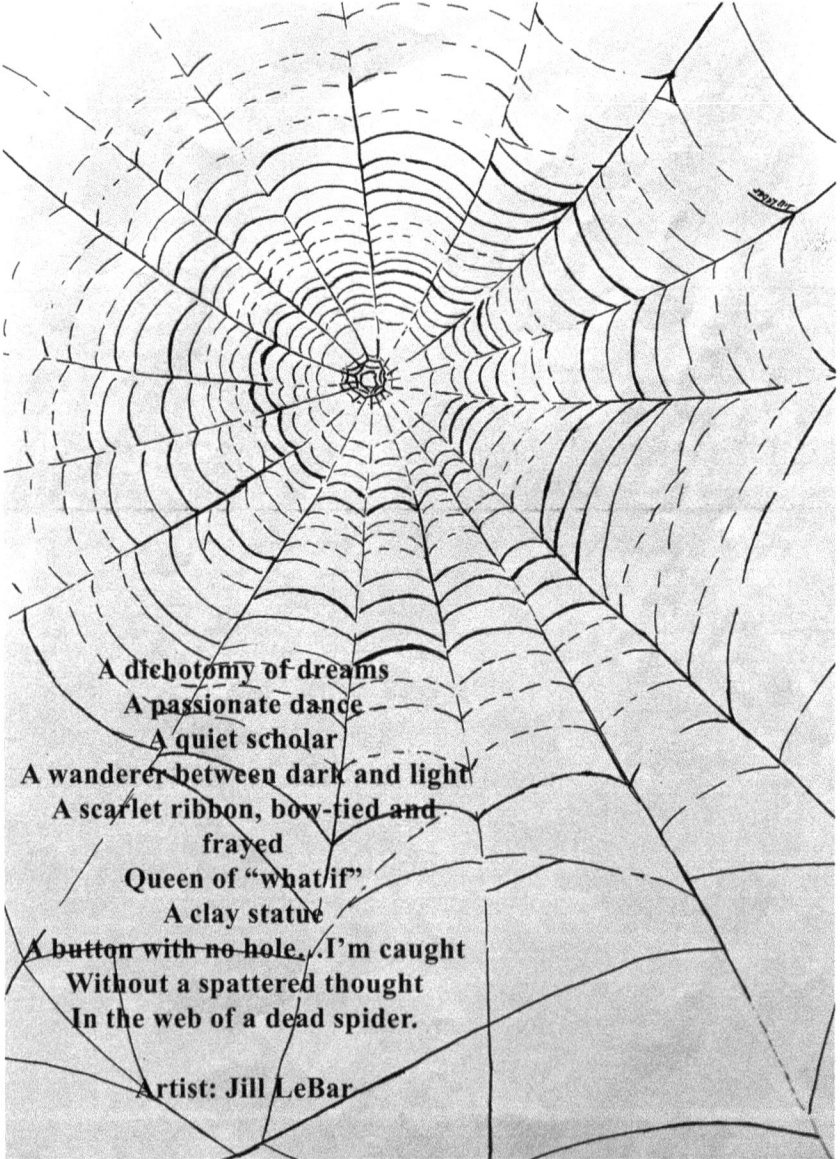

A dichotomy of dreams
A passionate dance
A quiet scholar
A wanderer between dark and light
A scarlet ribbon, bow-tied and
frayed
Queen of "what if"
A clay statue
A button with no hole...I'm caught
Without a spattered thought
In the web of a dead spider.

Artist: Jill LeBar

Introduction: The World Inside

In the secret recesses of our minds, hide the memories of the past, the hidden desires of the moment and the impossible dreams we can never give up. Sometimes a photograph, a written word, a look, or a shape projects these thoughts into the present. Whatever our senses touch upon, we seize for our metaphorical world. At times that metaphor flashes perception for ourselves or others. It is then that we wish to share it: such is the language of poetry. If, perchance, we have the good fortune to reach across the pages of time and space, then we might call ourselves a poet. For now, let us retrace.

"Attic Thoughts."

Attic Thoughts...
Vignettes of a Heritage

In calico thoughts, my spidery mind
Spins a taut pattern.
I gaze through my attic dormer,
Catching the blue-green frame of nightfall
On my dusty canvas.
A soft swirl plucking the leaves, reaches me,
The wind takes me back – AGES…

 I sit by the edge of a shallow pond,
 Drinking in the moist air.
 The muddy shoal of my skin
 Bends to touch the unwrinkled brow.
 I catch the breeze as it kindles art in brushed degrees.
 Prisms of sprinkled warmth hide
 My wrinkled, tawny feet.

 I watch the velvet night bend and stretch to a satin frieze.
 It catches the wind and heavy air,
 Curves in a delicate bow, dips low and tears free…
 By a fireside, I sit
 My red youth exploding into sparks,
 Disappears in the blank night,
 Then stretches to a candle glow.
 Inside the log, a wrinkled face waves goodbye.
 I warm my skin and wait…For the red and black edge to reach.
 I poke a cinder and move closer to the chill of ash.

In the glow of a shadow world
I whirl and fade in the tired rain that buckets dreams in a mirror game.
   I grow stiff and white in the pink light.
   I'm caught…
   Without a spattered thought
   In the web of a dead spider.

Thoughts of Self

"O wad some power the giftie gie us,
To see ourselves as others see us."
From "To a Louse" by Robert Burns

We like to think that we can indeed, see ourselves. Oftentimes, however, we see ourselves in others. These two poems are cameos of my grandmothers; each of them very different but loved equally. I would like to think that I can see something of myself in each of them. The first "Empty Benches" dedicated to MAMAW, my paternal grandmother who died at the age of eighty-one. The second is an image of my maternal grandmother who died at age ninety-five.

Empty Bench

An empty bench, a lonely tree,
The summer shade,
Grandmother and me.
Tracing patterns, wild and free,
Dancing daffodils, standing tall
Defiantly.
Grabbing moments in the sun
Catching laughter…
I run and hide,
Riding the wind of youth
Swinging wide, the gate of truth.
Her pride, jaded and rare,
Flits back and forth,
Beneath that tree.
No butterflies for me. Only the growing fear
Of empty benches
Lingering near
I understand her need to flee
The shade of a tree
For me.
The nothing that we share,
Jaded and rare: dancing silently.
An empty bench, a lonely tree,
The summer shade: Grandmother and me.

"Plummie"

At ninety-four, she reaches for the door.
Gentle, sane, a four-foot frame:
Humble, proud, tame,
"Plummie" is her name.
Blind: she leads the way,
Deaf: a whisper of yesterday,
Never missing rubles from her clan.
Breathing warbling notes, singing jaunty tunes,
Plucking up the rhythm of our age,
A wise sage, teasing time, along the climb.
Watching her, we learn
To shuffle at the door,
At ninety-four.

Rhythm of the Sea

"I must go down to the sea again, to the lonely sea and the sky."

– John Masefield "Sea Fever"

For me, the sea represents a beginning and ending. I began my life near the shores of the James River in the Tidewater, Virginia. Sights, smells, and sounds of the sea were part of those formative years. Later, as a resident of Downeast Maine, my memories are full of the beauty and breath of lakes, ponds, and coastlines where we hiked, sailed, and paddled in for forty-four years. This kaleidoscope of shapes and colors keeps rolling back to me: reflecting the tug-of-war between these two anchors.

Shells lie open in the sun
Pink flows slowly into white.
Once, it breathed and felt
Hiding the pearl no one could touch.
A train of sand, a torrid sun
Crept inside the life within.
This tug-of-war inside the tomb
Fed the sand and changed its worth.
A mind that drags the ocean depths,
  Searching for the kea
To unlock all the treasures
  In a land beyond the sea,
Will sink and fall below a line
  That lets in light and air;
Shutting out the world inside
  That drowns out all the care.

Walk Beside the Sea

I took one step
Crushed a hundred blades of grass,
Cutting a path to the rock.

Sitting on the mossy rock,
I watched green footprints
Sink into the brown.
I felt the ocean's tears.
I listened to the hollow waves,
Slapping cobwebs on my feet
Pulling the sand between my toes.

I dipped my hair into the foam,
Wrapped heavy strings across my arms
Waiting for the sting.
Licking the salt between my teeth,
I sucked in heavy air
That settled to my feet.

September in the Harbor

Warm, glowing, crisp
The wind stretches the white gauze
Over the pale blue sky
Autumn: green patches around the harbor
Interrupted here and there by tiny houses
Peering between the clusters of pine and birch,
Tucked neatly behind the last leaves of summer:
Gulls cry overhead.
Evening tide slaps gently on the smooth bellies of boats;
A tug of war: wind and tide
Pulling me inside
Adrift at close of day,
Letting go of harbor, dock and sky
A soft goodbye.

A Mountain Mist and I

A whisper lit the sky; turned our golden hay;
It wrapped the blackened stalks in cords of gray.
It settled in between the laughter and the fun;
No one could bring the sun.

We walked in silent avenues, parallels of fear;
The rhythm of our footsteps, a harmony of jeer.
Unless the shroud is lifted, our duet is done.
Someone lifts the corner; someone brings the sun.

In between the spaces, there fell a salty tear;
Not enough to drown the fire, nor cause the mist to clear.
Just enough to lift the heat; change the beat.
A mountain mist and I: said "Goodbye."

Growing Up

Growing up and in between:
A fence of black and white
Shadow of my other self
Walking behind.
Disappearing in the noontime
Returning in the afterglow
Of a culture gone astray.
Reclaiming friends of childhood:
      Josie's shadow in the hall
      A place embracing color
      Standing side by side with you.
Remembering Mom and Dad
      Warmth and wonder from the past
      Hugging one another in a color that is past.
In the glow of a shadow world
I whirl and fade in the tired rain
That buckets dreams in a mirror game
I grow stiff and white in the pink light…

He By She

HE buys me with his crooked smile,
    Trades me to a silent yesterday.
    A stealthy lad who toys and teases
    When he seizes,
    She he likes and guards and always pleases.
WE slip into his boyhood hide-and-seek,
    Tomorrow bends to childish play,
    Time is blocked.
    Locked in his sacred inner altar,
    My wounds have room to burn
    And I confess…
HIS funny crooked smile will someday yawn
    And into all that blackness I must crawl.
    Time will fill the coffer.
    I'll be left with just his smile to offer.

The Trap

Over my shoulder, I threw him a glance,
Not a come-on, merely a chance
To smile at someone (*it didn't matter who*)
Too innocent to reject,
Or inspect my cue.
Tripping along close at his heels
Was a Cocker Spaniel,
Barking approval and flapping his ears.
The scene was complete (it numbered three):
A girl, a boy, and a subtlety.

> *"Let's play a game; I'll be the wildcat*
> *You have to tame."*
> *"What about Skipper? Can he play too?"*
> *"Sure, bring him along. He'll be the hound*
> *Who tracks me down. I'll hide – Skipper will hunt.*
> *You'll have to collar me and fasten the chain."*

The game began; the girl is free. The hound is bound to the trapper's knee.
Next, he quickens his stride. The hound tilts his head, with defiant pride.
Quietly, he nears his prey; the hound is alert, even in play.
A leap through the air swift and sure!
The teeth of the hound are caught in the lure.
The boy bolts and screams at his dog.

> *"Skipper, let go! It's only a game. You've scratched her skin*
> *And made her bleed. If she's hurt, you're to blame."*
> *"I'm okay. Will you help me up?"*

The game ends; the girl is free.
The boy is bound to the trapper's plea.
Over his shoulder he turns to find
A whimpering spaniel, following behind.
Over her shoulder, she threw him a glance:
Not a come-on, merely a chance
To reject or trust (*It doesn't matter which*)
Either one is a bitch.

A Little Elf Passed My Way

A little elf passed my way
Stirred up my fancy and called me to play,
He led me in paths, narrow and green,
Teased me by hiding along mountain streams.

I followed because I was headed that way,
Shadows had beckoned the sunlight to stray.
The checkerboard forest was quiet that day –
Only the sound of the silence at bay.

Then the rim of my shoes tore a leaf at my feet.
I tripped quickly on tiptoe, to pad my retreat.
But the triangular hat of the elf at my side,
Tangled and ripped as I quickened my stride.

His hat was a guide to a giant like me –
A lively sail and a wonderful key.
Now I wait for my playmate to enter the room
And unlock this silence, here in my tomb.

In the Open Classroom

In the open classroom
    Space and Time are caught
    Expanding cells of energy
    That never can be bought.
Savor every moment
    Of these codicils of gold;
    Ignore the foolish fact
    That the body's growing old.
The blessings that it offers
    Are invisible to some.
    It's the whisper of potential
    That makes the journey fun.

Assignment 92

Before me, sit seven
Writing What?
Assignment 92.

"No, that won't do;
Write what you feel."

"But, I can't just peel
My emotions for you."

"Be honest.
Say what you think."

"I'm too tired to think."
"React."
(Now, I'm supposed to get
My electrons moving.
Hell. I can't move my body,
Much less my mind!)
"So, what do you expect of me"

"ASSIGNMENT 92."

After the Bell

The school bell rings:
The hall shatters,
And all that matters
Is ME.

I walk into the sun,
Looking for fun,
Swinging on the gate
Of liberty.

Don't tell me I'm young
And foolish and coy,
Or "Daddy's little boy."
I'm ME.

My father's history
Is not my style.
Yesterday's rules
Get me riled!
I'm free.

I stand up and fight
Regardless of place
Or time or space.
My hostility.
Give me a cause
And I will burn
The ancient laws
Of civility.

Fire is my will –
To make time mine
Someday I'll have to pay
The bill.

But today I'm free,
The payments are stalled.
Only a small fee
If I'm late.

This date is mine!
No return.
After the bell,
All that matters
Is ME!

Children of the Night

Staring at the sun,
The children run.
Blinded by the light,
They love the night.
One by one they come
To the altar of fun,
Sacrificing their goals
To pleasure's coals.
They bend their knees
To marijuana's fees,
And send their prayers
For angel dust fares.
They bless the dreams
Of opiate beams,
And wash away hope
By addition to dope.

Danny's Song

(A memorial for Danny, whose death one April morning affected me deeply. He was playing the king in our Drama class play; his moment on the stage was a major accomplishment and the cast was overwhelmed with grief and shock. The greater tragedy is our inability to understand his need, and reach the missing call for help.)

Alone, he died one April morn
    When he was seventeen.
His star-crossed eyes and swollen tongue
    Stared silent in the dirt.
He cried with all our hurt.

The tunes I listened to that day
    Blamed drugs and beer and friends
But no one claimed the dying breath
    A relative of his.
No faces shared the tears.

I wondered as the day wore on,
    What more I could have said,
What thoughts I should have tried to read
    Behind his staring eye,
A common grief or sigh?

I focused on scenes of yesterday
    When Danny played the king,
He mumbled words and missed his cue
    With others in his court.
The scene was much too short.

In church we heard the preacher's voice
    Rush through the litany
He never mentioned Danny's name;
    He never sang his tune.
The end came much too soon.

I wish the hours would hurry back,
    And redirect the scene,
Replay his role with a different voice
    Sung in a lower key,
Lengthen the melody.

The act was through,
I missed my cue,
All exited. The stage was bare,
The smell of flowers
Perfumed the air.

ALONE, he died one April morn
    When he was seventeen.
ALONE, he sings to a younger cast
    Who found him in the dirt,
With the echo of his hurt.

Graduation

Where have you been, my child?
    Walking the gilded path at early dawn.
    Stopping to pick the berries from the field
    Whistling at the moon, living my song.
What now, my child?
    The corpse of early years is laid to rest
    And with it go the flowers of the dawn.
    The dirge of Pomp and Circumstance is sung
    To quell the fear and praise the dying sun.
    The robe of green now covers up the grave,
    And heavy air brings down the mound of earth.
    The afternoon is yours to search and find,
    The richness of that death and life anew.
    No one can bring the morning back to life,
    Or paint it bright and change its greying hue.
What then, my child?
    Go make your sun,
    Light the evening fire,
    Gather morning dew,
    Whet your soul.
    Listen to the silence of your hour.
    Let it open up the door, to YOU.

To the Class of 2020

Today you begin a new path
      Leaving behind a web of images
            Carefree days of freedom and protection
                 Woven with cloth of childhood
                     The years of ups and downs
                           These are the memories of youth…

Forget and forgive all errors and moments of grief
      Rebirth and resolve to write a new leaf
            Full of energy, and belief in new turf
                 Ready for adventure and life on your own
                     Finding a voice in the open unknown…

Bury the burden of crisis and remake the present to fashion your dream
      Take hold of your beauty and boldness of self
            The knob of despair awaits the hand of passion
                 The wit of laughter and the flair of faith
                     Follow you wherever you walk and run

Grab every chance to "dance on…dance on…dance on…"
(Theodore Roethke)

– Graduation: May 2020

Poetry Is

Poetry is not words
It is an image
An art
That speaks to the heart
Like a dart
In ways that words do not.
It pierces; it stings;
It hurts, it sings
While it opens
Eyes to fears
To dreams
That drift and lift
A message
Beyond a sentence
Or theme.
A poem cannot be caught
In a trap of thought
Poetry is like the wind
That bellows and
Flows from within
To move its message
Across the sky
To blow and lift
A cloud of whim
Of the dark and dim
That rains giving life
To the grains of thought

That mold our minds
Moving a message
Across the earth
Binding us
Into humanity.

– Patricia Frech, 11/8/22

Appendix

The items in this section are directed to teachers/readers who may find them helpful in the classroom or for personal writing. Several documents in this section have been created by students as Samples. Please feel free to use this material for educational use.

Anglo-Saxon Riddle

- **Explanation of the genre and its origin**
- **Student samples: Zaniyah Diggs, Brett Deese**
- **Getting started: Writing a riddle**

Shakespearean Sonnet

- **Three lessons for imitating Shakespeare's style**
- **Samples of sonnets**

Self-Analysis: Personification of Self Using One Letter of Alphabet

- **Description of assignment**
- **Rubric**
- **Sample of personification presentation**

Models for Celebration of Self

- **Teacher Samples #1; #2**
- **Student Sample: Alan Fletcher**

Anglo-Saxon Riddles

Over the spam of five hundred years,
Disparate tribes and clusters of Angle-Saxons migrating to Britannia
Became one nation. Their literature and language grew
From an oral literature of lays, hymns, gnomes, history, songs and
Stories to a composite picture of a united kingdom, translated by
Alfred the Great in the *Anglo-Saxon Chronicles.*

The riddle as a genre found its way
Into mead halls and banquets and celebrations. The feature that appeals
to audiences today is the simplicity of the form and the complexity of its
wit. Our language, English, and its homeland (Anglo-land)
Has retained its Anglo-Saxon beginnings; however, as with any
language, it Merged during the Norman Conquest. Today it is a global
language. The riddle was popular then, and continues to this day.
Our students experimented with the genre, retaining the alliteration,
Personification, and kennings from the Anglo Saxons, and applied this to
Modern or universal elements.

I have a face, but no voice

My shape is round but not complete

I hang alone in a sea of dark

Watching you each night

Guiding you through the darkness

Pinned to the night

Scales in the sky

Ducking in and out the shuffles

Creating my own constellation

Magnificent mantle at midnight

Melting in midnight blues

Magnetically motivates

Moves modest phases

Wild waves weave together

Marvelous memories

Invocating presence

Glows golden

Fresh movement of melody

Strong and declaring

Yet, still and dazzling

Who am I?

– Zaniyah Diggs

I have a face, but no voice
My shape is round but not complete
I hang alone in a sea of dark
Watching you each night
Guiding you through the darkness
Pinned to the night
Scales in the sky
Ducking in and out the shuffles
Creating my own constellation
Magnificent mantle at midnight
Melting in midnight blues
Magnetically motivates
Moves modest phases
Wild waves weave together
Marvelous memories
Invocating presence
Glows golden
Fresh movement of melody
Strong and declaring
Yet, still and darling
Who am I

Getting Started
Writing the Riddle

First, think of an ordinary object that you are familiar with and can easily describe; for example, a book.
Next, think about what material the book is made of and put that in the first line, using the "I" to speak as the book:

I was born from the bark of a tree (*line has two b's [alliteration]*)
My lifeline is long if you treat me well,
And my shape and size may be large or small.
I provide entertainment without leaving your <u>wallstead</u> *(Anglo-Saxon word}*
My covers enclose battles, romances, adventures or facts.
I am your <u>silent-partner</u> when no one is near, *(original kenning)*
And I take you to places around the globe.
My back sometimes breaks if you drop me;
Sometimes I am left on my wooden bed without use,
I am bound by my leaves, but a tree I am not.
With age I will dry and my skin may fade.
Yet sometimes I last for more than a century
Hiding away in an attic or trunk.
My voice never fades if you find me unused,
Now use your <u>idea-bank</u> to guess my name. *(original kenning= [brain])*

Now Try Your Own Riddle:

Objects to consider: guitar, drum, basketball, boat, car, cellphone, TV, desk, bicycle, purse, chair, house, eyeglasses, baseball cap, etc...
[See list of Anglo-Saxon words; check elements of writing style for Anglo-Saxon sentences; review **Beowulf**]

Hear my howl, I whistle and move.

I am born from our star's blistering heat

Pressure gives me life from hot and cold.

Whether I am strong or weak, my existence is known.

My presence could be refreshing or rough.

I have no destination for my direction is random.

I birth the white among the blue in the sea.

When I reach the earth, I can create beautiful landmarks.

Transportation was my past purpose.

Men build mechanics to imitate me.

I only strengthen your woe in the winter.

You see my effect, but not me.

I can banish buildings with my strength.

Or I can foil your hair with my harshness.

I sprint pass your brow leaving less than a tickle.

I am harvested to turn the heat on in your house.

My counter slackens your speed as you move.

Measured by speed, but not by speedmeters.

Sky-pillows move along with me.

I am Mother Nature's soothing breath.

– Brett Deese

Brett Deese

Hear my howl, I whistle and move.
I am born from our star's blistering heat.
Pressure gives me life from hot and cold.
Whether I am strong or weak, my existence is known.
My presence may be refreshing or rough.
I have no destination for my direction is random.
I birth the white among the blue in the sea.
When I touch the Earth I can create beautiful landmarks.
Transportation was my past purpose.
Men build mechanics to imitate me.
I only strengthen your woe in the winter.
You see my effect, but not me.
I can banish buildings with my strength.
Or I can foil your hair with my harshness.
I sprint pass your brow leaving less than a tickle.
I am harvested to turn the heat on in your house.
My counter slackens your speed as you move.
Measured by speed, but not by speedometers.
Sky-pillows move along with me.
I am Mother Nature's soothing breath.

Sonnet Assignment

Students have been introduced to the sonnet genre; this assignment follows a reading of some of Shakespeare's sonnets and includes the elements for this genre. The meter is iambic pentameter, which is Shakespeare's meter. In order to help students with stress and the iambic line, students will practice recognizing "iambic".

Step one: Write out your first and last name; then divide the syllables by marking the stressed syllables with a diagonal line (/). See the sample below:

Name: Pa/ tri /cia / Frech / = 4 syllables; stress on tri and *Frech*

Since the second and fourth syllables are stressed; this

Line is *iambic* (unstressed, stressed)

Shakespeare's sonnets are written in *iambic pentameter* (which means that each line of poetry begins with an *unstressed* syllable, then ends with a stressed syllable.) Five *iambs* in a single line.

There are words in our language that are always iambic; for example, a few of these will always have a stress on the second syllable:

Away, upon, decide, reward, confine, within, into……

Read a line and "listen" to the stressed words to learn to recognize the meter (iambic pentameter). Read the following sonnet and listen to the iambic pentameter lines.

When I am sad, I walk beside the sea (*I , sad, walk, -side, sea) (stressed)*
Unstressed: *When, am, I, be-, the)*
The sea becomes at times a drawing board: Which syllables are stressed?
Stressed: *sea, -comes, times, draw, board*

SECOND SESSION: Today, write one quatrain (four lines) with 10 syllables in each; your sentence does not have to end at the end of the line; for example, the next line to the lines from Day One, wrap around;

The sea becomes at times a drawing board -/-/-/-/-/

Where I can trace out thoughts of you and me -/-/-/-/-/

<u>Second example:</u>
> *Along the way I watched the sunset weep*
> *(-long; way; watched; sun; weep); stressed syllables*
> *(A; the; I; the; -set); unstressed syllables*

Into the angry blue of waves and shore= - / - / - / - / - / (5 unstressed and 5 stressed)

Try writing four lines that compose a scene or a place......
Work on this first verse; tomorrow's lesson will outline Shakespeare's
Movement within the sonnet.

AT DUSK (sample quatrain)
Along the way, I watched the sunset weep
Into the angry blue of waves and shore
And standing midst the shadow underneath
A heron lifts its head to search and soar.
WRITING A SONNET: Third Session
Today, write two quatrains; then add a conclusion (final two lines)
SAMPLE: third quatrain and concluding summary (two lines = a couplet)
[Shakespeare's sonnets style]: three quatrains and a couplet.
And seals are swirling left and right to site
Those patterns in and out, a silver glow
That beckons them to follow moonbeams light,
To speed beneath the murky forest low.

The hunt is on—their bodies leap and roll;
An unexpected mass—within their reach
Defended only by a rocky knoll—
The seed of nature's storms upon the beach.
A darkened sky took up its space, and yawned
While creatures of the deep were gently spaw<u>ned</u>.
<u>Final couplet</u>: Shakespeare's pattern generally follows a form that moves from the descriptive to the analytical, or from the scene to a summary or finalizing line(s).

AT THE END OF CLASS TODAY, TURN IN YOUR SONNET; <u>DO NOT PANIC!</u>
THIS IS THE FIRST DRAFT: I WILL READ IT AND SHARE MY NOTES FOR
CONTINUING YOUR SONNET AND REVIEWING THE NEXT STEP.

Sonnets By the Sea

When I am sad, I walk beside the sea.
The sand becomes a drawing board
Where I can trace out thoughts of you and me.
I write your name; it binds me like a cord
To all the past I cannot now forgive:
To swollen dreams and talks beside the rocks;
To midnight swims we never shall relive;
To frozen moments underneath the docks.
That summer rushes back – the memories now roll
Like breakers rushing to a shifting shore.
The tide goes out and leaves a nameless shoal,
Ebbtide's silence returns an empty roar
And like the wind, I sift across this scene,
Erasing all you were and all you mean.

Egypt Bay, Maine

At dusk, I stand and listen to the sea:
The waves roar back and pound into my skin,
Recalling sights and scenes and mystery
That reign in summer's breath and autumn's wind.
The footprint of Katahdin, turning West,
A giant shadow moving with the sun
To face another day with naked breast,
Her regal nose untouched when day is done.
The pebbles on the shore heave with the tide,
Vibrating whispers back into the turf.
The squealing seals migrate; deer run and hide,
Relaying shafts of fear into the surf.
As foggy evening settles in the bay,
I shed my skin and slip away from day.

Self-Analysis
Goal of This Assignment

- To develop an analysis of yourself and turn it into a creative writing response
- To think outside the box
- Choose a letter of the alphabet that best defines your personality/character
- Use the literary device of personification to transform the "real" into an interesting and clever piece of writing
-Share this picture of "self" with an audience of your peers to inform, entertain, or delight your audience

Steps in the Process

- Select a letter of the alphabet that interests you and then list the physical and mental characteristics that match qualities of your personality
- Decide the qualities that relate to you in some way: physical, mental, or metaphorical
- List these descriptions, and divide them into categories such as appearance, related activities mental or physical
- Consider this letter to the position of other letters (before or after) if the position in the alphabet has some symbolic meaning
- Write a draft and share it with a peer for review/comments
- Revise and share with teacher for comments
- Create a visual picture of your analysis by either writing (artistically) or otherwise visually displaying your final product

NOTE: A sample is attached to this description; this sample is only one of many types; Feel free to be unique or clever or otherwise entertaining with your choice of presentation. The only caveat is that the end result must be appropriate for your classmates in this setting. Please speak to your teacher if you have any questions or reservations.

Personification
Self-Analysis

I am the letter "P"; fourteen letters
Ahead of me; ten behind me. I am proud
of my stance, and my back is straight and strong
but I am flexible because I loop
from the top of my body. My curves
are smooth, flattering, while my colleague
on my left is round, circular. My body
steals part of that loop; while my partner
on the right adds a small. Curved leg for stability
and originality; even though my position is solid
and free-standing, I recognize partnership with my
right; which symbolizes "correctness", adhering
to the rules. The straight-leg "Ps" and
"Qs" of my free-wheeling nature may
sound a bit proper or unyielding,
but I join with others to get the
job done: *prepare, present, and pro-
active*. This ability to initiate an
action or thought is an attribute
I am proud of, which brings
me to *pride of place, voice and
creativity*; I want students to be
creative, to engage their
brains, to predict and prepare.
Lastly, I rejoin my back,
keeping my feet on even keel.

RUBRIC FOR FINAL ASSIGNMENT: SONG OF MYSELF – Assignment

Each student will create an original poem about yourself. It will be upbeat and celebrate you and your accomplishments.

RUBRIC: Requirements:

_____Must have at least 25 lines; you may have more, but not less

_____Topic is yourself; celebrate yourself; must be upbeat

Only caveat is that it must be appropriate for the audience

_____Form: You may use rhyme; you may write in conversational style

You may create a particular form such as a ballad; you may create an original style; it must have rhythm but does not have to rhyme; it may have a "beat" or it may be soft and smooth.

The sample poems are written in the pattern of Walt Whitman's

Song of Myself. You may imitate this form or create your own.

_____Include poetic devices such as simile, metaphor, alliteration, or assonance or onomatopoeia or personification, imagery, etc.

You may imitate a ballad form or free verse; you may imitate a particular poet's style.

_____ Presentation: This is what the poem looks like: neatness,

print and position on the page; images *or illustration if used must be original [not cut and paste from online]. If* you choose to

artistically write this out, it must be neat and in ink (*no pencil*).

You may use a special font (be sure that it is a legible font).

You may center or create special spacing that fits the content.

Originality, creativity, and artistry.

This is your final assignment Due May 29, 2020

*Attached are two samples to get you started. The subject and form are up to you; use your own voice and celebrate accomplishments and/or personality/ traits.

Models for Celebration of Self
Celebration of Self #1

I sing of the things I love:
Places, people, and everyday things.
I love tomatoes and pizza and peach ice cream;
I love marshmallow cake and peanut brittle
And all things sweet and soft.

When I speak, I draw out my "O's";
When I listen, I lean out and reach every word.
When I shout, I make sure that the moment deserves it!
When I cry, it is all by myself in the night.
When I love, it surrounds me with arms that are tight.

My memory is the key to my family far away;
My foresight is my guide to a safe place to land;
My will is my strength 'cause it keeps me standing tall,
But my heart is my compass that finds my way home.
Together they are my package all folded and neat.

If the wind is too strong, and the heat is too hot,
If the rain thunders down in the middle of night,
If the cold wraps around me and chills me all through,
If the silence surrounds me and hushes my voice,
Then I scream 'till my body is bruised but not broken.
I know I can rise from a home that enfolds me.

I know I can count on my soulmate who comes to my side;
I know that my strength still comes from inside.
I know I can whisper and regain my pride –
Where my song of myself will always reside.

– Patricia V. Frech

Celebration of Self #2

Give me a note to dance and sing;
Give me laughter to lighten the night;
Give me a baseball to throw out the door;
Give me a hammer to pound out what's right.
Give me your promise to play me a tune.
Walk with me often, and run with the wind!
Gallop away to the ocean, and fly to the moon!
Find fun and fantasy in ordinary things,
Remember to jump and play with your dreams.
Say goodbye to the sadness and welcome the fun!
Travel light in the daytime and keep yourself warm.
Alone is not sadness; it's learning to live
Without fear and with wonder for another bright day.
Your mind is the map that will lead the way.
Make plans to escape when the walls close you in;
Develop resilience when boredom sets in.
Create your own castle in the middle of gloom;
Construct a soft landing with only a broom.
Come hop on my bike and we'll pedal the road
That winds through the hillside and down by the sea;
Remember the only wall we will face
Lies broken and cracked in the past we let go.
Nobody or nothing can hold us from glory.
Sing of a future we will never erase;
A blank wall we can paint any hue.
Our notes are jamming and blending
A song bold and new!

– Patricia V. Frech

The Bounds of Creation

I have always found great joy in creation
The manipulation of timber and metal,
The smoothness of stones and ivories,
The smoothness and vibrant colors of fabrics,
The softness and rarity of furs.

From the simple designs of culture come the complexity of manufacture,
The simplistic shine of iron transitions into the gilded masterpiece of steel.
From old and dead lumber come beautiful works of furniture,
From uncut rocks and bones come shining trinkets of finery,
From a long, still animal comes the warmth felt on a cold winter night.

But there are things which cannot be created by man's hands,
The great and silent mountains,
The wild and sprawling forests,
The lush and fertile oceans teaming with life,
The dry and shifting sands of the desert.
Farther still from man's manipulation lies something contained within his own heart

Something that drives him to either his best or his worst,
Something that lays down his selfishness for another,
Something that drives him or pushes no matter the cost,
That something which man contains, yet cannot create,

IS LOVE.

– Alan Fletcher (By permission of The Smithfield Times)

Printed in the USA
CPSIA information can be obtained
at www.ICGtesting.com
JSHW011327061223
52880JS00014B/52

9 798889 100386